L. V. Blum, United States Presbyterian Church, Presbytery of
Orange

Manual of the Presbytery of Orange

Containing the History, Standing Rules and the Rules of Parliamentary

Order, Revised and Adopted October, 1882

L. V. Blum, United States Presbyterian Church, Presbytery of Orange

Manual of the Presbytery of Orange
*Containing the History, Standing Rules and the Rules of Parliamentary Order,
Revised and Adopted October, 1882*

ISBN/EAN: 9783337163495

Printed in Europe, USA, Canada, Australia, Japan

Cover: Foto ©Lupo / pixelio.de

More available books at **www.hansebooks.com**

MANUAL

OF THE

PRESBYTERY OF ORANGE,

CONTAINING

THE HISTORY, STANDING RULES

AND THE

RULES OF PARLIAMENTARY ORDER.

Revised and Adopted October 1882.

SALEM, N. C.
L. V. & E. T. BLUM, BOOKSELLERS AND PRINTERS.
1883.

HISTORY.

I.—FORMATION. TERRITORY.

The Presbytery of ORANGE is the oldest of the existing Presbyteries in the Southern Church, and there are only four of the existing Presbyteries connected with the Northern Assembly that are older, viz: Philadelphia, New Castle, New York, and New Brunswick. In the order of formation, however, Orange was the *seventeenth* Presbytery formed after the sub-division of the Presbytery of Philadelphia in 1717.

The Orange Presbytery was set off from the Presbytery of Hanover, Va., in 1770, by the Synod of New York and Philadelphia. The first six named ministers on the roll given below, comprising the original Presbytery, were all members of the Hanover Presbytery. To these the Synod added a *seventh* member, viz: HEZEKIAH JAMES BALCH, distinguished for services rendered by him in the cause of civil liberty, as well as of Presbyterianism in North Carolina.

The first meeting of the Presbytery was held at the Hawfields in (then) Orange County, N. C., September 5, 1770. Rev. HENRY PATTILLO preached the opening sermon, and Rev. DAVID CALDWELL was appointed Stated Clerk.

The territory of the Presbytery extended indefinitely to the South and West from the Virginia boundary, but practically only the State of North Carolina, East of the Blue Ridge and the upper part of South Carolina, were occupied by its ministers.

There was, at a very early period, a Presbytery in
South Carolina and Georgia, which had no eccle-
siastical connexion with the Synod, and, as in the
case of Messrs. JAMES CAMPBELL and JAMES ED-
MONDS, *ninth* and *tenth* on the roll, ministers were
occasionally received from that body into Orange.
(Records of the Presbyterian Church, pp. 409. 451.
Howe's His. of Presb. Church in So. Carolina.)

It is a matter of deep, though vain regret that
the Records of the Presbytery, embracing the first
twenty-five years of its existence are lost; also,
the Records covering the interval from 1812 to
1827,—a gap altogether of forty years. This fact
rendered the preparation of the following Roll of
Members, from the beginning in 1770, a less easy
task than it would have been otherwise. All
available collateral sources of information have
been used, but still it is probable that there are
omissions of unknown names, and it is certain
that many of the earlier dates can only be approx-
imated. The changes which have occurred since
the organization, in territory, boundaries, &c., to
the present time, will be noted at their proper
place in the following Historical Roll of the Presbytery :

II. ROLL OF MEMBERS.*
From the formation to the present time.

Entered.		Left.
1770	HUGH MCADEN, *Hanover,*	*1781
"	HENRY PATTILLO, *Hanover.*	*1801
"	JAMES CRISWELL, *Hanover.*	
"	DAVID CALDWELL, *Hanover.*	*1824
"	JOSEPH ALEXANDER, *Hanover*	1785
"	HEZEKIAH BALCH, *Hanover.*	1775
"	HEZEKIAH JAMES BALCH, *Donegal.*	*1777

* The names in *italics* annexed to names of members show
the Presbyteries from which they severally came into Orange
as ordained ministers; those in roman letters the Countries.

5

Entered.		Left.
1771-1774	JOHN HARRISS, *Lewston*	1785
"	JAMES CAMPBELL, *South Carolina*	*1781
"	JAMES EDMONDS, *South Carolina*	1785
"	THOMAS REESE	1785
"	JOHN SIMPSON	1785
1775-1776	ALEXANDER McMILLAN, Foreign........Deposed	1776
1777	SAMUEL E. McCORKLE	1795
"	THOMAS H. McCAULE	1795
"	JOHN DEBOW, *New Brunswick*	*1783
"	THOMAS HILL	1785
1778	ANDREW PATTON, Asso. Ref. Penna	
"	JAMES HALL	1795
"	ROBERT ARCHIBALD...............Deposed	1797
"	JOHN COSSAN	1787
1779-1784	ALEXANDER McWHORTER, *New York*	1781
"	THOMAS CRAIGHEAD	1787
"	JAMES McREE	1795
"	JAMES TEMPLETON	1785
"	DANIEL THATCHER	1790
"	JAMES FRAZIER	1784
"	FRANCIS CUMMINS	1785
"	DAVID BARR	1795
1784-1787	JACOB LAKE	1794
"	JOHN BECK	

In 1784 the Presbytery of SOUTH CAROLINA was set off by the Synod from Orange Presbytery. The following members of the Presbytery met at the Waxhaws, South Carolina, April 1785, and held their first meeting, viz: JOSEPH ALEXANDER, FRANCIS CUMMINS, JAMES EDMONDS, JOHN HARRISS, THOS. REESE and JOHN SIMPSON. The State line between North and South Carolina became the southern boundary of Orange.

———.

States, or Denominations whence received; and all names without such designation are names of members who became such by ordination in the year prefixed to their names. A * placed before the date on the right hand indicates removal by death in that year. Where no date is given in this column it means either that it is unknown, or that the person is still a member, which may be readily ascertained from the Roll of Churches. The figure in ( ) following a name denotes membership the *second* or *third* time, of the same person.

1789	DAVID KERR, Ireland	1796
1790	WILLIAM MOORE, *Hanover*	1801
1792	WILLIAM HODGES	1800
"	JAMES WALLIS	1795
"	SAMUEL C. CALDWELL	1795
"	COLIN LINDSAY, Scotland........Deposed	1803
1793	LEWIS F. WILSON	1795
"	JAMES McGREADY	1796
"	JOSEPH D. KILPATRICK	1795
"	ALEXANDER CALDWELL	1795
"	ANGUS McDEARMID, Scotland......Deposed	1803
1794	SAMUEL STANFORD	1812
1795	JOHN ROBINSON	1801
"	JAMES H. BOWMAN	1815
"	HUMPHREY HUNTER, *South Carolina*	1795
"	JOHN MAKEMIE WILSON	1795
"	JOHN CARRIGAN	1795
"	WILLIAM McGEE	1795
"	WILLIAM L. THOMPSON	1802

In 1795 the Presbytery of CONCORD was set off from Orange by the Synod of the Carolinas. The Yadkin River was made the line of division, Concord embracing the territory West, and Orange, East of this line. After the division the following ministers composed Orange Presbytery, viz: PATTILLO, CALDWELL, MOORE, McGREADY, BOWMAN, HODGES, LINDSAY, ROBINSON, STANFORD, KERR, and McDEARMID.

1798	JOHN GILLESPIE	1810
"	SAMUEL McADOO	1801
"	WILLIAM PAISLEY	*1857
1799	JOHN ANDERSON	1801
"	ROBERT TATE	1812
1802	LEONARD PRATHER, Methodist Church	
"	DANIEL BROWNE	1809
1803	JOHN MATTHEWS	1806
"	ANDREW FLINN	1805
"	MALCOM McNAIR	1812
"	EZEKIEL B. CURRIE	*1851
1804	MURDOCK McMILLAN	1812
"	HUGH SHAW	1812
1806	JAMES SMYLIE	1812
1808	WILLIAM L. TURNER, *Lexington*	1812
"	JAMES K. BURCH	1810

1809 JOHN McINTYRE.. 1812
" MURDOCK MURPHY, *1st Pres. of So. Ca*.................. 1811
1810 WILLIAM McPHEETERS, *Lexington*...................*1836
" WILLIAM B. MERONEY...
1811 JOSEPH CALDWELL..*1835
1812 BENJAMIN H. RICE... 1812
" JAMES W. THOMPSON..................................*1816
" ALLEN McDOUGALD.. 1812
" WILLIAM PEACOCK.. 1812
" 'SAMUEL PAISLEY... 1836

In 1812 the Synod of the Carolinas set off the Presbytery of FAYETTEVILLE from Orange, South of the following line: Mouth of Neuse River to junction with Trent River, thence direct to junction of Deep and Haw Rivers, thence direct to mouth of Uharrie River on the Yadkin. The following ministers composed the new Presbytery, viz: STANFORD, TATE, TURNER, McNAIR, McMILLAN, McINTYRE, MERONEY, McDOUGALD and PEACOCK. Mr. MERONEY, however, having removed out of the bounds of the new Presbytery before its first meeting was never actually a member. This year the Synod of the Carolinas was dissolved, and the year following the Synod of North Carolina, comprising the Presbyteries of Orange. Concord and Fayetteville, held its first meeting at Alamance church.

1813 ROBERT H. CHAPMAN, *Troy*............................... 1816
1816 JONATHAN OTIS FREEMAN................................. 1821
1817 JOHN WITHERSPOON... 1833
" JOHN H. PICKARD..*1858
" JAMES MORRISON.. 1819
1818 SHEPHERD K. KOLLOCK.................................. 1825
1821 SAMUEL L. GRAHAM... 1836
" LEMUEL D. HATCH.. 1834
" ELISHA MITCHELL.......................................*1857
" ELI W. CARUTHERS.....................................*1865
1822 ARCHIBALD D. MONTGOMERY............................ 1852
1823 STEPHEN FRONTIS... 1828
1824 FREDERICK FREEMAN....................................... 1824
" JAMES W. DOUGLAS.. 1834
1825 JESSE RANKIN... 1827

1826 JOSEPH LABAREE, *Champlain* 1829
" ELIJAH GRAVES, ——————? 1842
1826 JAMES WEATHERBY 1834
" JAMES KERR 1826
" JOHH KNOX 1829
1827 EDWARD HOLLISTER, Coos Assoc. Vermont 1834
" WILLIAM NEILL 1835
" DARIUS C. ALLEN 1829
" THOMAS LYNCH 1827
" WILLIAM S. PLUMER 1831
" ROBERT H. CHAPMAN (2), *Winchester* 1827
1828 DANIEL A. PENICK, *Hanover* 1836
" ABNER W. GAY, *Fayetteville* .... Deposed 1831
" SAMUEL H. SMITH 1831
1827 THOMAS P. HUNT, *Hanover* 1831
" HIRAM P. GOODRICH, *Albany* 1838
" NEHEMIAH H. HARDING 1836
" MICHAEL OSBORNE, *Elizabethtown* 1835
" SIDNEY WELLER, *Assoc. Ref. Pres. of N. Y.* 1836
1830 ALEXANDER WILSON 1836
1831 DANIEL L. RUSSELL, *West Hanover* 1835
" JESSE RANKIN (2), *Concord* 1836
" GEORGE W. FERRILL 1839
" ALBERTUS L. WATTS 1835
1832 GEORGE C. CHESLEY, Methodist Church 1835
" PHILLIP PEARSON 1836
1833 THOMAS LYNCH (2), *Western District* *1869
" JOHN S. MCCUTCHEON 1835
" SAMUEL HURD, *West Hanover* 1833
1834 SAMUEL J. PRICE 1835
" DRURY LACY, *East Hanover* 1836
" WILLIAM MCELROY *1837
" JAMES D. HALL 1837
1835 THOMPSON BIRD, *Newburyport* 1840
" JAMES PHILLIPS *1867
" WILLIAM P. FORREST 1835
" JOSEPH A. GRAY 1836
" WILLIAM A. SHAW 1836
" DANIEL G. DOAK 1847

In 1835 the Synod of North Carolina set off in the eastern portion of Orange, by a line running along the western boundaries of the counties of Granville and Wake, a new Presbytery, styled the Presbytery of ROANOKE. The following members of Orange resided within said limits at the time, viz: MCPHEETERS, GRAHAM, RANKIN, HARDING,

WELLER, WILSON, LACY, GRAY and SHAW. The
first meeting was held in Washington, N. C., March
31, 1836, and was opened with a sermon by the
Rev. Dr. S. L. GRAHAM.

1833 NEHEMIAH H. HARDING (2), *Roanoke*..................*1849
" ALEXANDER WILSON (2), *Roanoke*..............*1867
" ROBERT BURWELL, *East Hanover*............... 1858
" NATHANIEL B. PATTERSON.........................*1837
1837 JOHN A. GRETTER, *East Hanover*..............*1853
" JONATHAN T. ELY................... 1843
1838 SAMUEL PAISLEY (2), *Concord*.................... 1838
" BENJAMIN M. SMITH, *West Hanover*.............. 1840
1839 JESSE RANKIN (3), *Roanoke*................... 1842
" JOHN C. RANKIN................... 1842
" WILLIAM N. MEBANE.........................*1859
" DANIEL STRATTON, *Roanoke*................... 1852
" THOMAS R. OWEN, *Roanoke*................... 1859
" GEORGE W. FERRILL (2), *Roanoke*...................
" SAMUEL H. SMITH (2), *Roanoke*...................*1843
" DRURY LACY (2), *Roanoke*................... 1855
" SAMUEL L. GRAHAM (2), *Roanoke*................... 1842
" WILLIAM McPHEETERS (2), *Roanoke*...................*1843
" JOHN C. THOMPSON, *Roanoke*...................*1841
" SIDNEY WELLER (2), *Roanoke*................... 1841
" GEORGE D. McCUEN, *Philadelphia* 1844
" SAMUEL J. P. ANDERSON................... 1846

In 1839 the Presbytery of Roanoke was dissolved and its ministers, churches and territory
were reunited to Orange by the Synod of North
Carolina.

1840 JOHN WITHERSPOON (2), *Harmony*..................*1853
1841 JOHN PAISLEY *1845
1842 EDWARD HINES *1879
1843 JACOB DOLL................... *1878
" ANDERSON G. HUGHES................... *1873
" WILLIAM C. SUTTON................... 1848
" EDMUND C. BITTINGER................... 1864
1845 GILBERT MORGAN, *Albany*................... 1851
1846 ARCHIBALD CURRIE...................
1847 J. B. McBRIDE................... 1847
" WILLIAM V. WILSON, *West Hanover* 1852
" CYRUS K. CALDWELL................... 1867
1848 JAMES N. LEWIS, *Montgomery*................... 1854
" S. ADDISON STANFIELD *1874

1849 JAMES STRATTON, *East Hanover* 1854
"   MONROE T. ALLEN, *Western District* 1852
"   NELSON Z. GRAVES 1860
1850 JOHN S. GRASTY 1856
"   WILLIAM B. BROWNE 1851
"   JAMES H. MCNEILL, *Fayetteville* 1855
"   SAMUEL H. WATKINS, *West Hanover* 1853
1851 ROBERT LOGAN 1852
1852 F. N. WHALEY, *Winchester* 1866
"   THOMAS U. FAUCETTE ....
1854 THOMAS G. WALL, *Winchester* 1862
"   WILLIAM P. WHARTON *1856
"   JOHN M. SHERWOOD 1861
1855 JOHN M. KIRKPATRICK, *East Hanover* 1866
"   J. JONES SMYTHE, *Fayetteville* 1859
"   JOHN W. MONTGOMERY 1866
"   JOSEPH M. ATKINSON, *Baltimore* ....
1856 JOHN I. BOOZER, *South Carolina* 1858
1857 PLEASANT H. DALTON, *Concord* ....
"   WILLIS L. MILLER 1867
"   DANIEL MCGILVARY 1859
1858 P. ARTHUR MCMARTIN, *West Jersey* 1867
"   THOMAS B. NEILL, *Cherokee* 1863
1859 JOHN B. SHEARER 1866
"   J. HENRY SMITH, *West Hanover* ....
"   EPHRAIM H. HARDING 1866
1859 FRONTIS H. JOHNSTON ....
"   DONALD E. JORDAN 1882
1860 ANDREW D. HEPBURN, *Lexington* 1875
"   ROBERT J. GRAVES 1866
1861 DRURY LACY (3), *Concord* ....
"   WILLIAM A. WOOD, *Concord* 1866
"   JAMES C. ALEXANDER ....
1862 JOHN C. COBLE, *Louisiana* 1863
"   CALVIN N. MORROW ....
"   HENRY B. PRATT, *Cherokee* 1865
1865 HALBERT G. HILL 1868
1866 CALVIN H. WILEY ....
"   CHARLES PHILLIPS ....
"   WILLIAM B. TIDBALL, *Roanoke* ....
"   LACHLAN C. VASS, *West Hanover* ....

In 1866 the General Assembly transferred that portion of the territory of Orange lying in the State of Virginia South of Dan River, to the Synod of Virginia, to be attached to the Presbytery of Roanoke. The ministers transferred were Messrs.

KIRKPATRICK, WHALEY and SHEARER; with the churches of Danville, Clarksville, Spring Hill and Penuel. The State line then became the boundary line.

1867	HENRY B. PRATT (2), *Concord*.....................	1879
"	DANIEL T. TOWLES, *Bethel*..................	1870
1868	JOHN M. M. CALDWELL, *Concord*.............	1871
1871	EPARAIM H. HARDING (2), *Concord*...........	1874
"	JAMES W. SHEARER.................	1872
"	WILLIAM C. SMITH................	1873
"	P. TINSLEY PENICK, *Montgomery*...........	1876
1872	JOHN W. PRIMROSE................	
"	ROBERT BURWELL (2), *Mecklenburg*...........	
1873	CHARLES M. PAYNE................	1874
"	JAMES H. FITZGERALD, *West Hanover*...........	1881
"	WILLIAM G. BAIRD................*1878	
1874	E. M. GREEN, *Augusta*............	1877
1875	WILLIAM A. SHAW (3), *Brazos*...........	1880
"	HENRY T. DARNALL, *East Hanover*..........	
"	CORNELIUS MILLER...........	1882
"	THOMAS J. ALLISON...........	
1876	JAMES L. CURRIE...........	
"	J. MONROE ANDERSON, *Concord*...........*1879	
"	SAMUEL M. SMITH	
1877	WILLIAM R. ATKINSON, *Roanoke*...........	1879
"	ROGER MARTIN, *Montgomery*...........	1878
"	PATRICK R. LAW...........	
1878	JOHN S. WATKINS, *Roanoke*...........	
"	B. WATKINS MEBANE...........	1881
1879	DAVID C. RANKIN, *Savannah*...........	1880
"	D. IRVIN CRAIG...........	
1880	LUCIUS H. BALDWIN, *Newark*...........	1882
"	ANDREW M. WATSON, *Memphis*...........	
1881	GEORGE SUMMEY, *Ebenezer*...........	
"	R. A. WAILES	
1882	SAMUEL L. WILSON, *Bethel*...........	
"	JAMES L. WILLIAMSON, *Bethel*...........	

Total of Members 221.

III.—PERMANENT OFFICERS.

With date, as far as known, of appointment and retirement.

STATED CLERKS.

1770	DAVID CALDWELL.................	1776
1776	JAMES CRISWELL.................	
	THOMAS H. McCAULE.................	
	JAMES McGREADY.................	1796

1796 JAMES H. BOWMAN... 1803
1803 WILLIAM PAISLEY...
     JOHN WITHERSPOON... 1827
1827 JAMES W. DOUGLAS... 1831
1831 SAMUEL L. GRAHAM... 1835
1835 N. H. HARDING.. 1848
1848 JACOB DOLL.. 1878
1878 F. H. JOHNSTON........................... *Winston, N. C.*

TREASURERS.

1797 WM. HODGES.. 1803
1803 LEONARD PRATHER... 1809
1809 MURDOCK McMILLAN...
     ELISHA MITCHELL...
     L. D. HATCH... 1830
1830 N. H. HAREING... 1835
1835 N. C. READ (R. E.)... 1836
1836 WILLIAM C. McELROY.. 1836
  " E. W. CARUTHERS.. 1841
1841 DRURY LACY.. 1850
1850 JOHN A. GRETTER... 1853
1853 JESSE H. LINDSAY (R. E.)............ *Greensboro, N. C.*

IV.—ROLL OF CHURCHES.

*According to organization, with name and address of
Minister and Clerk of Sessions.*

1. GRASSY GREEK. 1753 (about).

Rev. J. W. PRIMROSE, Pastor, Oxford, N. C.
Dr. G. A. Wilson, Sassafras Fork, N. C.

2. HAWFIELDS. 1755.

.... Vacant.
S. K. Scott, Mebanville, N. C.

3. RED HOUSE. 1755.

Rev. T. U. FAUCETTE, S. S., Milton, N. C.
John P. Rainey, Milton, N. C.

4. ENO. 1755.

Rev. JAMES L. CURRIE, Pastor, Chapel Hill, N. C.
N. D. Bain, Hillsboro, N. C.

5. GRIER'S. ——.

.... Vacant.
Thomas Smith, Hightower, N. C.

6. BUFFALO. 1756.

Rev. James C. ALEXANDER, Pastor, Greensboro, N. C.
....

7. NUTBUSH. 1757.

.... Vacant.
R. A. Bullock, Williamsboro, N. C.

8. SPEEDWELL. 1759.

.... Vacant.
.... No Session.

9. LITTLE RIVER. 1761.

Rev. JAMES L. CURRIE, Pastor, Chapel Hill, N. C.
John H. Terry, Caldwell Institute, N. C.

10. ALAMANCE. 1762.

.... Vacant.
Joseph W. Gilmer, Gilmer's Store, N. C.

11. BETHESDA. 1765.

Rev. D. I. CRAIG, S. S., Reidsville, N. C.
A. S. Williamson, Ashland, N. C.

12. STONY CREEK. 1770.

.... Vacant.
J. L. Wilson, McCray's Store, N. C.

13. BETHLEHEM. 1770.

Rev. T. J. ALLISON, Pastor, Bingham's School, N. C.
D. F. Morrow, Oaks, N. C.

14. CROSS ROADS. 1792.

.... Vacant.
B. F. White, Mebaneville, N. C.

15. NEW HOPE. ——.

Rev. P. H. DALTON, S. S., High Point, N. C.
J. T. Hogan, University Station, N. C.

16. BETHEL. ——.

Rev. JAMES C. ALEXANDER, Pastor, Greensboro, N. C.
....

17. CHAPEL HILL. ——.

Rev. JAMES L. CURRIE, Pastor, Chapel Hill, N. C.
Prof. F. P. Venable, Chapel Hill, N. C.

14

18. RALEIGH FIRST CHURCH.
Rev. JOHN S. WATKINS, Pastor, Raleigh, N. C.
W. S. Primrose, Raleign, N. C.

19. HILLSBORO. 1816.
Rev. JAMES L. WILLIAMSON, Pastor, Hillsboro, N. C.
John Norwood, Hillsboro, N. C.

20. NEWBERN. 1817.
Rev. L. C. VASS. Pastor, Newbern, N. C.
George Allen, Newbern, N. C.

21. OXFORD. 1818.
Rev. JOHN W. PRIMROSE, Pastor, Oxford, N. C.
M. V. Lanier, Oxford, N. C.

22. WASHINGTON. 1822.
Rev. SAMUEL M. SMITH, Pastor, Washington, N. C.
C. M. Brown, Washington, N. C.

23. GREENSBORO. 1825.
Rev. J. HENRY SMITH, DD., Pastor, Greensboro, N. C.
Jesse H. Lindsay, Greensboro, N. C.

24. MILTON. 1826.
Rev. T. U. FAUCETTE, S. S., Milton, N. C.
Dr. W. L. Stamps, Milton, N. C.

25. LEXINGTON. 1827.
.... Vacant.
Wm. B. Hammer, Lexington, N. C.

26. WARRENTON. 1828.
.... Vacant.
.... No Session.

27. LOUISBURG. 1832.
.... Vacant.
.... No Session.

28. SHILOH. 1832.
Rev. J. W. PRIMROSE, Pastor, Oxford, N. C.
N. V. Watkins, Sassafras Fork, N. C.

29. FAIRFIELD ——.
Rev. A. CURRIE, S. S., Hillsboro, N. C.
J. N. Clark, Hillsboro, N. C.

30. YANCEYVILLE. 1858.
.... Vacant.
R. B. Watt, Yanceyville, N. C.

31. PITTSBORO'. 1848.
Rev. P. R. LAW, S. S., Pittsboro, N. C.'
John A. Womack, Pittsboro', N. C.

32. ASHBORO'. 1850.
.... Vacant.
A. C. McAllister, Ashboro', N. C.

33. GRAHAM. 1850.
Rev. GEORGE SUMMEY, Pastor, Graham, N. C.
W. C. Donnell, Graham, N. C.

34. MADISON. 1857.
.... Vacant.
Wm. B. Carter, Madison, N. C.

35. GENEVA. 1852.
Rev. GEORGE W. FERRILL, S. S., Tally Ho, N. C.
John H. Webb, Tally Ho, N. C.

36. OAKLAND. 1858.
Rev. ROBERT BURWELL, D. D., S. S., Raleigh, N. C.
B. W. Young, Leachburg, N. C.

37. MT. AIRY. 1858.
.... Vacant.
Wm. F. Carter, Mt. Airy, N. C.

38. HIGH POINT. 1859.
Rev. P. H. DALTON, Pastor, High Point, N. C.
W. C. Denny, High Point, N. C.

39. WENTWORTH. 1860.
.... Vacant.
Thomas A. Ratliffe, Wentworth, N, C.

40. HAYWOOD. 1860.
Rev. P. R. LAW, S. S., Pittsboro', N. C.
J. H. Mann, Lockville, N. C.

41. LEAKSVILLE. 1860.
.... Vacant.
George W. Peay, Leaksville, N. C.

42. HOREB. 1861.
.... Vacant.
.... No Session.

43. OAK HILL. 1862.
.... Vacant.
N. B. Daniel, Oak Hill, N. C.

44. WINSTON. 1862.
Rev. F. H. JOHNSTON, Pastor, Winston, N. C.
Thomas J. Wilson, Winston, N. C.

45. MEBANENILLE. 1868.
Rev. T. J. ALLISON; Pastor, Bingham School, N. C.
Robert Bingham, Bingham School, N. C.

46. HENDERSON. 1868.
.... Vacant.
Samuel Watkins, Henderson, N. C.

47. SPRING WOOD. 1868.
.... Vacant.
A. G. Clapp, Gibsonville, N. C.

48. DURHAM. 1871.
Rev. H. T. DARNALL, Pastor, Durham, N. C.
W. H. Hanks, Durham, N. C.

49. OREGON. 1874.
.... Vacant.
W. K. Davis, Oregon, N. C.

50. TARBORO'. 1874.
Rev. R. A. WAILES, Pastor, Tarboro', N. C.
....

51. REIDSVILLE. 1875.
Rev. D. I. CRAIG, Pastor, Reidsville, N. C.
J. M. Andrews, Reidsville, N. C.

52. ELKIN. 1875.
.... Vacant.
.... No Session.

53. MT. VERNON. 1876.
Rev. P. R. LAW, Pittsboro', N. C.
J. A. Houston, Ore Hill, N. C.

54. RALEIGH SECOND CHURCH.
Rev. JOSEPH M. ATKINSON, D. D., Pastor, Raleigh, N. C.

55. LITTLETON. 1877.
Rev. S. L. WILSON, S. S., Littleton, N. C.
Dr. R. A. Patterson, Littleton, N. C.

56. OAK FOREST. 1879.
Rev. D. I. CRAIG, Pastor, Reidsville, N. C.
Wm. Ferguson, Ruffin, N. C.

57. ROCKY MOUNT.
Rev. R. A. WAILES, Pastor, Tarboro', N. C.
O. R. Sadler, Rocky Mount, N. C.

58. COMPANY SHOPS. 1879.
Rev. GEORGE SUMMEY, Pastor, Graham, N. C.
John Anderson, Company Shops, N. C.

59. NAHALAH. 1880.
Rev. S. L. WILSON, S. S., Littleton, N. C.
Dr. M. T. Savage, Scotland Neck, N. C.

60. JAMESTOWN. 1881.
Rev. P. H. DALTON, S. S., High Point, N. C.
William Wiley, Jamestown, N. C.

61. CALAH. 1881.
.... Vacant.
P. K. Foust; Foust's Mills, N. C.

62. GULF. 1882.
Rev. P. R. LAW, S. S., Pittsboro', N. C.
J. M. McIver, Gulf, N. C.

63. CROATAN. 1882.
Rev. S. H. ISLER, S.S., (Presb. Wilmington,) Goldsboro, N. C.
W. H. Bray, Newbern, N. C.

Ministers without Charge.
Rev. DRURY LACY, D. D., Jonesboro, N. C.
Rev. Prof. CHARLES PHILLIPS, D. D., Chapel Hill, N. C
Rev. C. H. WILEY, D. D., Supt. A. B. S., Winston, N. C.
Rev. C. N. MORROW, Hartsville, Tenn.
Rev. W. B. TIDBALL, Greensboro, N. C.

Licentiates.
BOSWELL B. PALMER, (c) Milton, N. C.
WM. F. THOM, Greensboro', N. C.

V.—GENERAL DOCKET.

1. Prayer.
2. Roll Call.
3. Moderator and Clerks chosen.
4. Minutes of last Session read.
5. Excuses of Absentees.
6. Appoint the following Committees :—
    1. On Narrative to the General Assembly, and the Synod.
    2. On Minutes of the Synod.
    3. On Minutes of General Assembly (Fall).
    4. On Systematic Benevolence. Rule 16 (3).
    5. On Reports of Sessions on Sessional Duties.
    6. On Sessional Records. (4 Committees.)
    7. On Treasurer's Account.
    8. On Devotional Exercises.
    9. On Installations. Rule 16 (8).
7. Are there any new candidates?
8. Are there any candidates to be examined? If so,
9. Appoint an Elder on each of the Examining Committees.
10. Devotional Exercises *second* day at 10 o'clock.
11. Reports of Sessions
    1. State of Religion. Read.
    2. On Sessional Duties. Referred.
    3. On Systematic Beneficence. Referred.
    4. On Sabbath Schools. Referred.
12. Reports of Permanent Committees, Agents,&c.
    1. Executive Committee of Education.
    2. Agent of Home Missions.
    3. Evangelists.
    4. Supplies appointed at last meeting.
    5. Agent of Sabbath Schools. (Spring.)
    6. Agent of Foreign Missions. (Fall.)
    7. Agent of Publication. (Fall.)
    8. Licentiates.

9. Treasurer. (Spring.)
10. Trustees of Presbytery.
11. Trustees of Davidson College. (Fall.)
12. Commissioners to Gen. Assembly. (Fall.)
13. Committee on Assessments.
14. Examining Committees.
13. Reports of Standing Committees,
  1. At Spring meeting, on Narrative; Systematic Benevolence; Sessional Duties; Sessional Records; Minutes of Synod; Treasurer's Account; Devotional Exercises; Installations.
  2. At Fall meeting on Minutes of General Assembly; Devotional Exercises; Installations.
14. Appoint Agent of Home Missions. (Spring.)
15. Read Historical Sketches.
16. Nominate Commissioners to General Assemsembly. (Spring.)
17. Elect Commissioners to General Assembly. (Spring.)
18. Time and Place of next Meeting.
19. Read and Correct Minutes.
20. Adjourn with Singing, Prayer and Benediction.

STANDING RULES.

SECTION I.—GOVERNMENT.

RULE 1. The Rules of Parliamentary Order adopted by the General Assembly of the Presbyterian Church in the United States are hereby adopted as Standing Rules for the Government of this body. (See Manual, page 35.)

RULE 2. All Standing Rules shall be introduced with these, or some such words, to denote that they are Standing Rules, viz: "*Resolved*, That it be a standing rule, &c., &c."

RULE 3. It shall require *two-thirds* of all the members present to suspend, amend, or abolish a standing rule.

SECTION II.—CHURCH SESSIONS.

RULE 4. It is the duty of every Church Session to appoint representatives, principal and alternate, to all the meetings of the Presbytery and Synod; and in no case will the Presbytery enroll the name of a representative who has not been regularly appointed by his Session. The representative who first takes his seat as member, whether principal or alternate, shall, ordinarily, sit in all the adjourned meetings of the court, following the regular stated meeting. In the case of an adjourned meeting of the Presbytery during the session of Synod, the Session should specifically appoint the representative Elder in the Synod to sit also as member of the Presbytery, unless he be already a member of the Presbytery by enrollment at its last stated meeting.

RULE 5. Church Sessions are required to present their Records annually at the Spring meeting of the Presbytery, for the purpose of review.

RULE 6. Each Session is required to forward

annually to the Presbytery, at the Spring meeting, a written narrative of the State of Religion in the bounds of the congregation, to be read in the Presbytery, and thereafter placed in the hands of a Committee to prepare a narrative for the General Assembly and the Synod.

RULE 7. The particular subjects to be embraced in the narrative shall be the following, with such additional matter as the Session may deem important or proper to show the spiritual growth or decline of the church, viz: Fidelity of Ministers, Elders and Deacons; -Attendance of the People upon Public Worship; Prayer meeting; Observance of the Sabbath; Family Worship; Monthly Concert of Prayer for Missions; Bible Classes; Sabbath School; Religious Instruction of the Coloured People; Number of Conversions and Additions to the Church by Profession; and, lastly, Systematic and Regular Contributions for the various Benevolent Schemes of the Church as conducted by the General Assembly and the Presbytery.

RULE 8. Each Session is required to report in writing annually to the Presbytery at the Spring meeting whether (a) Provision is made for the Poor of the Church, so that none are dependent on public charity; (b) Representatives are appointed as required (Rule 4); (c) Provision is made for defraying the traveling expenses of Representatives and Ministers to the Presbytery and Synod; (d) They have punctually paid their assessments and apportionments to the various Presbyterial Funds and the salary they have agreed to pay heir Minister.

RULE 9. In each case in which a church reports a failure to pay punctually to its Minister the salary promised, the church so failing shall be summoned to appear by its representatives or commissioners before the Presbytery, and show cause for such failure.

RULE 10. The Presbytery will entertain no call from, and grant no supplies to any church in arrears for ministerial services rendered, except in cases in which satisfactory reasons are presented to the Presbytery.

RULE 11. Ministers and Congregations have no right to change the conditions of a call, and the Presbytery will recognize no such alteration.

RULE 12. The Presbytery asserts and maintains its authority over the relation of Stated Supply. It can be formed only by the consent of Presbytery, and it can be continued only by a new application to the Presbytery at every Spring meeting, or in the interim it may be formed or continued by the Agent of Home Missions, subject to the endorsement of the Presbytery. The relation of Stated Supply shall, in all cases, terminate on the 31st of March each year.

RULE 13. Every church shall report and transmit promptly to the Treasurer of Presbytery all monies collected for the Benevolent Causes of the Church as ordered by the General Assembly.

RULE 14. Sessions shall give their careful attention to the provisions of the Book of Discipline, Chap. XV., Par. 2, 3 and 4, respecting the transfer of non-resident members; and they shall always report the whole number of registered communicants to the Presbytery, and not merely the number residing at the time in the bounds of the congregation.

RULE 15. Clerks of Sessions shall fill out all the blanks sent by the Stated Clerk of Presbytery, and after their approval by the Session, they shall forthwith return them to the Stated Clerk.

Section III.—Presbyterial Committees.

(Classed as Standing, Executive and Examining.)

Standing Committees.

RULE 16. The following Committees shall be appointed at every Spring meeting of the Presbytery, viz:

1. To prepare a narrative for the General Assembly and the Synod, based upon the written reports of the Sessions.

2. To examine and report on the reports of Sessions on Sessional Duties.

3. To prepare a report for the General Assembly, and to examine and report on the reports of Sessions, on Systematic Beneficence, (*a*) noting the omission of any collection ordered by the General Assembly, (*b*) examining reasons assigned for the omission, and recommending judgment thereon, approving or disapproving, as the case may be. (And it shall be the duty of the Stated Clerk to endorse these judgments when adopted by the Presbytery, on the reports, and return them to the churches respectively.)

4. To review the records of Sessions. For this purpose the roll of Churches shall be divided into four sections, and a Committee appointed to each section.

5. To examine the Minutes of Synod and report any matters therein requiring the attention of the Presbytery, and at the Fall meeting a similar Committee shall be appointed to examine and report on the Minutes of the General Assembly.

6. To audit the Treasurer's Account.

7. To arrange for the Public Worship and other devotional Exercises which the Presbytery may appoint to be held.

8. To make arrangements for Installations.

(These last two Committees shall be standing Committees at every stated meeting.)

EXECUTIVE COMMITTEES.

Education.

RULE 17. The Presbytery will conduct the cause of Education in accordance with the General Assembly's plan, and an Executive Committee shall be appointed to act in concert with the Assembly's Committee.

RULE 18. This Committee shall be charged with the oversight of all the unlicensed candidates under the care of the Presbytery. They should keep themselves informed of their deportment, diligence and progress, religious as well as literary, by correspondence with professors of the College and Seminary; and by judicious inquiry of Ministers, Elders, or other persons, endeavor to ascertain their profitableness for the ministry while engaged in teaching, mission work, colportage, or such like occupations during their intervals of literary study. They are required also to recommend the continuance of every candidate who is a beneficiary, as such, or not, according to their judgment; and they shall report annually at the Spring meeting, in full, of all this matter of their superintendence.

RULE 19. No candidate shall receive aid from the Education Committee before he places himself under the care of the Presbytery.

Assessments.

RULE 20. The Agent of Home Missions, Stated Clerk and Treasurer of this Presbytery shall be a permanent Committee on Assessments. It shall be their duty from time to time to revise the schedule of Assessment and Apportionment to the Presbyterial and Evangelistic Funds; to recommend increase or reduction in special cases; and to fix the amounts on new churches, subject always to the approval of Presbytery.

RULE 21. The Presbytery shall be divided into eight Committees (permanent) on the examination of candidates, and when the Presbytery has convened the Moderator shall have power to fill all vacancies for the time being, and to appoint a Ruling Elder on each of the Committees.

RULE 22. These Committees shall have assigned to them the following subjects in their order, for the examination of candidates, viz:

First Committee: Geography, Ancient and Modern; General History.

Second Committee: Latin; Latin Exegesis; Critical Exercises.

Third Committee: Greek; Hebrew; Logic.

Fourth Committee: Mathematics; Elements of the Physical Sciences, as Natural Philosophy, Chemistry, Astronomy, Geology, &c.

Fifth Committee: Mental Philosophy; Moral Science.

Sixth Committee: Theology, Natural and Revealed,

Seventh Committee: Ecclesiastical History.

Eighth Committee: Church Government; Sacraments.

The Committees Nos. 1, 2, 3, 4 and 5 shall conduct their examinations privately, and report to the Presbytery their recommendations; but the remaining Committees shall conduct their examinations in open Presbytery, after which each member of the Court shall have the opportunity to ask questions.

RULE 23. The Minister of the congregation within whose bounds the Presbytery may meet, shall be required to have such books in readiness as may be necessary for the above examinations.

SECTION IV.—PRESBYTERIAL AGENTS.

Home Missions.

RULE 24. The Presbytery will appoint annually at its Spring meeting one minister to be called the Presbyterial Agent of Home Missions, whose duty it shall be to have the oversight and conduct of the missionary work within its bounds, in accordance with the General Assembly's plan, and under the regulations of its Executive Committee.

RULE 25. This Agent shall include in his charge Sustentation proper; the relief of disabled Ministers, and families of deceased Ministers; Church extension; and the nomination of supplies to vacant churches. He shall report in full of all his operations at every Stated meeting.

RULE 26. This Agent shall also make every effort which in his judgment may seem practicable, to supply the vacant churches and missionary fields with the regular ministry of the Word, and to secure systematic and liberal contributions to the Sustentation cause from every church and missionary station in the Presbytery.

Publication.

RULE 27. The Presbytery shall appoint one of its members to look after the interests of the Publication cause within its bounds, and to be corresponding member of the Assembly's Committee. He shall also have the supervision of Colportage work in the bounds of the Presbytery, and it shall be his duty to look out and employ, whenever the Presbytery deems it expedient, suitable agents to carry our books to the doors of our people, and to distribute tracts, Bibles and small volumes among the ignorant and destitute throughout the Presbytery.

Foreign Missions and Sabbath Schools.

RULE 28. A presbyterial Agent of Foreign Missions, and another of Sabbath Schools shall be appointed in response to the resolutions of the General Assembly.

RULE 29. The Agents of Foreign Missions and Publication shall make an annual report in writing on the subjects of their Agencies at the Fall meeting; and the Agent of Sunday Schools at the Spring Meeting.

RULE 30. These various Agents and Committees are instructed to draw on the Treasurer for an amount sufficient to defray the expenses of their respective agencies.

Trustees.

RULE 31. The Presbytery shall elect a " Board of Trustees of Orange Presbytery," which board shall be composed of five persons who are members in good and regular standing in the Presbyterian Church, and shall hold in trust for the Presbytery all property in church lots and buildings, not otherwise secured, and all legacies and bequests which may be willed to the Presbytery in behalf of charitable and other objects under its control.

RULE 32. This Presbytery accepts the proposition of Concord Presbytery to take part in the government of Davidson College, and will regularly, at the proper times, elect Trustees of that Institution.

Section V.—Missionary and Evangelistic Labor.

Rule 33. The Presbytery shall be divided into two missionary fields by the following lines, viz: the eastern boundaries of Caswell, Alamance and Chatham counties, each to be occupied by an Evangelist as soon as competent support can be guaranteed.

Rule 34. The attention of the Evangelist shall be directed first to the vacant churches of his field, and then to other points of interest as he may have opportunity, unless otherwise specified by the Presbytery, or in the interim of its meetings, by the direction of the Agent of Home Missions.

Rule 35. The Evangelist is recommended,

(a) To hold at least once a year protracted services at his various preaching places, and especially, and if possible, more frequently at the more promising points.

(b) To organize weekly prayer-meetings and Sabbath schools wherever it is possible.

(c) To acquaint himself with the condition and wants of his field, with the persons and families therein so far as possible; and by his social and christian intercourse, by the distribution of Bibles and other religious books and tracts, and by the circulation of the Church papers, and by any other proper means within his reach, endeavor to disseminate the knowledge, and spread the influence of Scriptural religion and Gospel truth.

And he shall make a full report, in writing, of his labors, and the prospects of doing good in his field, to the Presbytery at each Stated meeting.

Rule 36. In order to raise the necessary funds for the support of the Evangelist, each church shall be apportioned a definite sum proportioned as nearly as possible to its ability, and the fund so formed shall be known as the "Presbyterial Evangelistic Fund." At the same time all the Ministers of the Presbytery are urged to recommend the cause to the attention of persons of means, and to the zeal and co-operation of Christian women.

RULE 37. Any missionary church or station persistently refusing or neglecting to contribute to the Evangelistic Fund shall forfeit all claim to the special benefits which this plan is designed to secure.

SECTION VI.—LICENTIATES.

RULE 38. When a candidate for the ministry is licensed to preach the Gospel, the Moderator shall, in the name of the Presbytery, present him with a copy of the Holy Scriptures.

RULE 39. All licentiates under the care of this Presbytery shall be assigned to suitable fields of labor, and they are required to be present at its Stated meetings, and to give an account of their labors.

RULE 40. If a licentiate is necessarily absent from a Stated meeting, it shall be his duty to send a written report of the manner in which he has been occupied. But if a licentiate absent himself without report or excuse for two years from the meetings of the Presbytery, his license shall be recalled.

SECTION VII.—PRESBYTERIAL OFFICERS.

Moderator.

RULE 41. In choosing a Moderator the persons to be voted for shall first be nominated. After the nominations are all made, the roll is to be called by the Stated Clerk, and no person is to

be voted for unless he has been previously nominated. A plurality of the votes shall decide the
election.

RULE 42. At each Stated meeting the Moderator shall call on all Ministers present who are
marked as absentees, to state their reasons for
previous failure to attend. If no motion is made
expressive of disapprobation, the reasons assigned
shall be deemed satisfactory.

Stated Clerk.

RULE 43. The Stated Clerk shall keep on hand
a supply of all such blanks as may be necessary to
made Sessional reports to the Presbytery and
Presbyterial reports to the General Assembly.
He shall send to each Church Session between
the *first* and *tenth* days of March of each year all
the necessary blanks for reports of Sessions, viz :
Statistical, Sessional Duties, Systematic Beneficence, Sabbath Schools and any other that may
be ordered.

RULE 44. The Stated Clerk shall be required
to write to each of the delinquent churches, and
inform them of the amount of their debts and
request payment.

RULE 45. The Stated Clerk shall send a copy
of the Docket of the Presbytery to the Pastor of
the church where it is to convene, at least one
week previous to the time appointed for the
meeting.

RULE 46. He shall cause the Minutes of each
Stated meeting to be published with such excep-
tions as a majority of the Presbytery may direct ;
and when the Minutes are printed in pamphlet
form, he shall send a copy of the same to the
Treasurer and to the " Presbyterian Historical
Society" for preservation.

RULE 47. The Stated Clerk shall have charge of the business of making arrangements with the various railway companies for reduced rates of travel to members of the Presbytery attending its meetings.

Treasurer.

RULE 48. The Presbytery will raise annually by assessment on the churches a fund to be called the Presbyterial Fund. Of this fund the Treasurer shall pay annually,

(*a*) To the Contingent Fund of the General Assembly the annual assessment on this Presbytery.

(*b*) The annual traveling expenses of its Commissioners to the General Assembly.

(*c*) The contingent expenses of the Presbytery as, the Salary of the Stated Clerk; Postage; Printing the Minutes; Quota of this Presbytery to the Contingent Fund of the Synod; Expenses of the various Agents and Committees of the Presbytery; Traveling Expenses of the Trustees of Davidson College from this Presbytery; and for whatever other purpose the Presbytery may direct.

RULE 49. The Treasurer shall procure and forward by mail, as soon as published, a copy of the Minutes of the General Assembly of each year, to every Minister and Licentiate in the Presbytery.

SECTION VIII.—MISCELLANEOUS.

RULE 50. A portion of the morning, commencing at 10 o'clock of the *second* day of the stated sessions of the Presbytery, shall be spent in devotional exercises.

RULE 51. During the stated sessions of the Presbytery recess shall be taken for the purpose of attending worship with the congregation.

RULE 52. Whenever a Minister of this Presbytery is removed by death, a Committee shall be appointed to prepare a sketch of his life and character, which shall, after approval, be recorded in a book of Biographical sketches, kept for that purpose by the Stated Clerk.

RULE 53. From time to time as may seem expedient the Presbytery shall have historical sketches of its churches prepared, and copies thereof deposited with the Presbyterian Historical Society of Philadelphia for preservation.

RULE 54. Commissioners to the General Assembly shall be nominated at least one day before the election.

PARLIAMENTARY RULES.

Of Opening the Sessions.

1. The Moderator shall take the chair precisely at the hour to which the court stands adjourned ; shall immediately call the members to order ; and on the appearance of a quorum, the session shall be opened with prayer.

2. If a quorum be assembled at the hour appointed, and the Moderator be absent, the last Moderator or oldest minister present, shall take the chair without delay.

3. If a quorum be not assembled at the hour appointed, any two members shall be competent to adjourn from time to time, that an opportunity may be given for a quorum to assemble.

4. After calling the roll, and marking the absentees, the minutes of the last sitting shall be read, and if requisite, corrected.

Of the Moderator.

5. It shall be the duty of the Moderator to preserve order, and to conduct all business before the court to a speedy and proper result.

6. He is to propose to the court every subject of deliberation that comes before it.

7. He may propose what appears to him the most regular and direct way of bringing any business to issue.

8. He shall always announce the names of members rising to speak, prevent them from interrupting each other, and require them in speaking, always to address the chair.

9. He shall prevent a speaker from deviating from the subject, and from using personal reflections.

10. He shall silence those who refuse to observe order.

11. He shall prevent members leaving the court without his permission.

12. He shall, when the deliberations are ended, put the question, and call the vote.

13. In all questions he shall give a clear and concise statement of the object of the vote, and the vote being taken, he shall declare how the question is decided.

14. He shall carefully keep notes of the orders of the day, and call them up at time appointed.

15. He may speak to points of order in preference to other members, rising from his seat for that purpose, and shall decide questions of order subject to an appeal to the court, without debate, by any two members.

16. If any member consider himself aggrieved by a decision of the Moderator, it shall be his privilege to appeal to the court and the question on such appeal shall be taken without debate.

17. It is his duty to appoint all committees except in those cases in which the court shall decide otherwise.

18. When a vote is taken by ballot, or by yeas and nays, he shall vote with the other members; in other cases, when the court is equally divided, he shall possess the casting vote. If he be not willing to decide, he shall put the question a second time, and if the court be again equally divided, and he decline to give his vote, the question shall be lost.

19. He may call any member to the chair, to preside temporarily.

Of the Clerk.

20. As soon as possible after the commencement of the first session of every court, the Clerk

shall form a complete roll of the members present, and put the same into the hands of the Moderator; and whenever any additional members take their seats, he shall add their names in their proper places to the said roll.

21. He shall immediately file all papers in the order in which they have been read, with proper endorsements, and keep them in perfect order.

Of the Order of Business.

22. After the reading of the minutes of the preceding day, the following order of business shall be observed:

First—The receiving of

    a Communications addressed to the body;
·   *b* Reports of standing Committees;
    c Reports of select Committees;
    d Resolutions; each of which papers may, by unanimous consent, be taken up immediately on presentation, but if objection be made it shall be docketed.

Secondly—The unfinished business in which the court was engaged at the last preceding adjournment, in preference to orders of the day; but such unfinished business may, on motion without debate, be laid on the table, to proceed with the special order.

Thirdly—As soon as the special order and the unfinished business are disposed of, the business on the docket will be called; but motion to elect officers, to appoint committees, and to enroll members, shall always be in order, unless a member is speaking, or the court is voting.

Of Motions.

23. A motion must be seconded, and afterwards repeated by the Moderator, or read aloud,

before it is debated; but this shall be no bar to explanations of the object of any motion by the mover, provided he does not exceed five minutes; and every motion shall be reduced to writing, if the Moderator or any member require it.

24. The mover of a resolution is entitled to the floor if he so desire, after the Moderator has stated the question.

Of Withdrawal of Motion.

25. Any member who shall have made a motion shall have liberty to withdraw it with the consent of his second, before any debate has taken place thereon, but not afterwards without the leave of the court.

Of Limitation of Debate.

26. Motions to lay on the table, to docket, to take up business, and to adjourn, and the call for the question, shall be put without debate. On questions of order, postponement or commitment, no member shall speak more than once. On all other questions, each member may speak twice, but not oftener without express leave of the court.

Of Privileged Questions.

27. When a question is under debate, no motion shall be received unless to adjourn, to docket, to lay on the table, to amend, to postpone indefinitely, to postpone to a day certain, or to commit; which several motions shall have precedency in the order in which they are herein arranged; and the motion for adjournment shall always be in order.

Of "the Question."

28. When any member shall call for "the question," the Moderator shall, without debate, put the

present, the vote shall immediately be taken on
the pending question, whatever it may be, without further debate.

Of Division of Question.

29. If a motion under debate contains several
parts, any two members may have it divided, and
a question taken on each part.

Of Amendments.

30. An amendment may be moved on any question, as also an amendment to the amendment,
which shall be decided before the original proposition; but two distinct amendments to the pending question shall not be entertained at the same
time, whether moved as substitutes for the whole
matter, or as changing any part thereof.

31. One proposition may be substituted for another, when the substitute covers the whole matter
of the original, and this shall be done by moving
to strike out the original, and insert the substitute.

Of Reconsideration.

32. A question shall not be reconsidered at the
same sessions of the court at which it has been
decided, unless by the consent of a majority of the
members who were present at the decision, and
unless the motion to reconsider be made by a
person who voted with the majority.

33. A subject which has been indefinitely post-
poned shall not be again called up during the same
sessions of the court, unless by the consent of
three-fourths of the members who were present
at the decision.

Of Speakers.

34. If more than one member rise to speak at

the same time, the member who is most distant from the Moderator's chair shall speak first.

35. Every member, when speaking, shall address himself to the Moderator, and shall treat his fellow members, and especially the Moderator, with decorum and respect.

Of Interruptions.

36. No speaker shall be interrupted unless he be out of order, or for the purpose of correcting mistakes or misrepresentations.

Of Voting.

37. Members shall not decline voting, unless excused by the court.

38. When various motions are made with respect to the filling of blanks with particular numbers or times, the question shall always be first taken on the highest number and the longest time.

39. When the Moderator has commenced taking the vote, no further debate or remark shall be admitted, unless there has evidently been a mistake; in which case the mistake shall be rectified and the Moderator shall recommence taking the vote.

40. The yeas and nays on any question shall not be recorded, unless it be required by one-third of the members present; and every member shall vote "yea" or "nay" unless excused by the court. In a judicial case, members thus excused shall not be allowed to vote in any of the subsequent proceedings relating thereto.

41. In all elections it shall require a majority of the votes cast to elect.

Of Committees.

42. The person first named on any committee shall be considered as the chairman thereof, whose

duty it shall be to convene the committee and preside therein; and in case of his absence or inability to act, the second named member shall take his place and perform his duties.

Of Private Sessions

43. All courts have a right to sit in private on business which, in their judgment, ought not to be matter of public speculation.

Of the Committee of the Whole.

44. Every court has a right to resolve itself into a committee of the whole, or to hold what are commonly called *interlocutory meetings*, in which members may freely converse together without the formalities necessary to their ordinary proceedings. In all such cases the Moderator shall name the member who is to preside as chairman. If the committee is unable to agree, a motion may be made that the committee rise, and upon the adoption of such a motion the Moderator shall resume the chair, and the chairman of the committee shall report what has been done, and ask that the committee be discharged, which being allowed, the matter shall be dropped. If the committee shall agree upon the report to be made, or have made progress in the same without coming to a conclusion, the committee may rise, report what has been done, and if the case require, may ask leave to sit again; or the committee of the whole may be dissolved, and the question considered by the court in the usual order of business.

Of Decorum.

45. Without express permission, no member of a court, while business is going on, shall engage in private conversation; nor shall members address one another, nor any person present, but through the Moderator.

46. When more than three members of the court shall be standing at the same time, the Moderator shall require all to take their seats, the person only excepted who may be speaking.

47. If any member act in any respect in a disorderly manner, it shall be the privilege of any member, and the duty of the Moderator, to call him to order.

48. All expressions of approbation or disapprobation, by clapping of hands or stamping, or any audible applause, shall be considered disorderly. (Adopted by Assembly of 1874.)

49. No member shall retire from any court without the leave of the Moderator, or withdraw from it to return without the consent of the Court.

Of Cases unprovided for.

50. All cases that may arise, not provided for in the foregoing rules, shall be governed by the general principles of parliamentary law.

Of Closing the Session.

51. The Moderator of every court, above the church session, in finally closing its sessions, in addition to prayer, may cause to be sung an appropriate psalm or hymn, and shall pronounce the apostolic benediction.

www.ingramcontent.com/pod-product-compliance
Lightning Source LLC
Chambersburg PA
CBHW021432090426
42739CB00009B/1460